Acknowledgments Many individuals contributed valuable time posing, barking, urinating, eating dog biscuits, and behaving badly in the making of this book. I would like to thank the following (and especially their owners) for their hard work and patience: Ben, Chena, Sammy, Web, Breaker, Lady, Grace, Hope, Mitchell, Millie, Scout, Jake, Ruby, Cooper, Schmidty, Mattie, Gunny, Midge, Tucker, Lincoln, Bella, Charlie, Chance, Sesame, Decker, Kit, Cousa, Cuma, Cole, Brillo, Snuffy, Lizzie, Bell, Lance, Shay, Dave, Joe, Sassy, Maggie, Jenny, Jimmy, Diamond, Merle, Tobi, Marley, Spike, Keno, Buck, Leilu, Sparky, Powder, Rabbit, Fancy, Cutter, Ozzy, Quest, Flicka, Kota, Buddy, Kristi, Sherman, Yorke, ridgid, MacGregor, Hale Bopp, Malakki, Pasha, Katy, Spot, Bonnie, and Snoopy.

Special thanks to my Muse and good friend, Roper Green—sorry, no Tiffany box ou—and to Susan Ewing, whose friendship and editing pen are greatly appreciated. This s dedicated to Griz and Sparky, who inspired many ideas in this book.

blished by Willow Creek Press, P.O. Box 147, Minocqua, Wisconsin 54548

Design by Patricia Bickner Linder

Library of Congress Cataloging-in-Publication Data
Buckley, Bill
e stupid : after all, they're man's best friend! / by Bill Buckley
p. cm.
ISBN 1-57223-395-8 (alk. paper)
Humor. 2. Dogs--Caricatures and cartoons. I. Title.
PN6231.D68 B83 2000
818'.602--dc21   00-011031

Printed in Canada

Dogs Are Stupid

B
for y
book

Pu

Dogs o

1. Dogs

W
P

MINOCQUA, W

Dogs Are Stupid

(After all,
they're man's
best friend!)

by
Bill Buckley

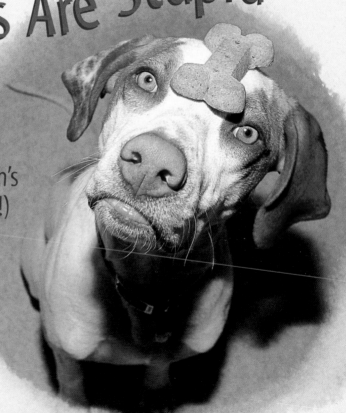

Part One

Stupid is
as stupid does

Here are a few reminders in case you haven't watched Rover lately. Whatever your excuse for thinking he might actually be smart, perhaps a glimpse into his everyday world will change your mind.

Sniffing butts is hardly the mark of intelligence.

O
ne man's garbage is a dog's meal.

The simpler the pleasures, the simpler the mind.

Dogs are fascinated by human eating rituals.

Dogs cannot be trusted with their own well being and are sometimes made to suffer certain indignities. Luckily, indignation is a concept they can't grasp.

Just like many men, dogs are preoccupied with bodily functions.

12

A fly can get
the better
of a dog
for hours.

Balancing a tennis ball on one's nose takes exceptional concentration and skill. Letting someone balance it there, well, that takes an exceptionally uncomplicated mind.

Think about it—he actually can't wait to get that slimy, grimy tennis ball in his mouth.

Dogs never let what you're doing interfere with what they're doing . . .

...However, what they do can certainly interfere with what you're trying to do.

Think of this the next time you're buying premium dog food.

An animal that lives to retrieve a piece of plastic, whenever it is thrown and for however long you can throw it, can't be terribly bright.

n some ancient cultures, men rolled in manure to express abject grief. Dogs do it simply because they like it.

Even the tiniest, eensiest crumb can spellbind a pooch.

t is believed that where dogs mark their territory, the most dominant one pees last....

That it's an endless cycle of one-upmanship
never occurs to a dog.

24

To a dog, size is a state of mind.

You might enjoy this for the first half-dozen times. Bet you will never find out how long it takes your dog to get bored with it.

Dogs like to lie down where they'll be most in the way.

It's easy to be brave
when the enemy
can't reach you.

The power of a dog treat cannot be overestimated.

32

A dog bent on playing catch knows no bounds.

The grass is always greener on the other side of the door ... although once there, a dog can't tell why.

34

s it stupidity or a clever campaign to wear you down?

D rooling isn't usually
associated with
intelligence.

Every dog is in touch with his "inner child."

S elf-expression isn't always desirable in a dog.

41

Give a dog some rope, and while he may not hang himself, he'll certainly try.

43

44

Dogs don't know what's good for them, but they know what tastes good.

How many Labs does it take to retrieve a training bumper?

The threat to one's domain can come from the strangest places.

Put a dog bred to catch rodents in a room with a hamster cage—step back and enjoy the show.

G ot dirt?

Play with your dogs and you've entertained them for a day; teach them how to play by themselves and you've entertained them for life.

52

f a Lab's brain is the size of a walnut, a Dachshund's is the size of a pea. If you're not convinced, get a laser pen.

M arking one's territory may seem pretty straight-forward,

but territory can be a difficult concept for a dog to grasp.

"**M**ake yourself at home" is one thing you never have to tell a dog.

t may look like just nose prints to you, but from his perspective it's a great work of art.

Most dogs have never heard about Greeks bearing gifts.

A dog's version of looking at life through rose-colored glasses.

Part Two

Takes one
to know one

Living with dogs means having to perform all sorts of unpleasant tasks and tolerate all manner of disgusting and irritating behavior. Which says one of two things: Either we are so needy we'll do anything for companionship, or we're stupid too.

People who feel superior to their dogs probably shouldn't look in the mirror.

s there any other
species on the
planet that does this
for another species?

T he best intentions can
backfire on you.

Your dog and you will never agree on body scent.

Living with a dog offers many opportunities to practice Zen.

Fleece blanket, $40; mounted duck, $185; Lamp shade, $50; new area rug with piddle on it, worthless.

Your puppy. Don't leave home without him.

Would you let your boyfriend do this?

Hating yourself for your own stupidity won't bring back your groceries.

No matter how fast you run or how loudly you yell "No!", they're gonna get you every time.

Leadeth your dog not into temptation.

A^{hh, the pleasure of solitude and a good book ...}

Ahh, the pleasure of solitude and a good book ...

Ahh, the pleasure of solitude and a good book ...

A lazy man always has practical applications for his dog.

S ome dogs just
don't get it…

and neither do their owners.

Sometimes just having a dog is a good enough trick.

D
ogs and kids' minds work on the same level:
Do whatever it takes to get to dessert.

A nd a good time was had by all.

A dog is definitely man's best friend, but some dogs' friends severely test the relationship . . .

O f course, on the road, the proper wardrobe is a necessity, not simply a statement.

Man's best friend taken to extremes.

The family that
sings together,
stays together.

They're just dogs ... Really.

You don't even have to own a dog to go bonkers about one.